# Highways

by Chris Bowman

BLASTOFF!
2
READERS

BELLWETHER MEDIA • MINNEAPOLIS, MN

Note to Librarians, Teachers, and Parents:

**Blastoff! Readers** are carefully developed by literacy experts and combine standards-based content with developmentally appropriate text.

**Level 1** provides the most support through repetition of high-frequency words, light text, predictable sentence patterns, and strong visual support.

**Level 2** offers early readers a bit more challenge through varied simple sentences, increased text load, and less repetition of high-frequency words.

**Level 3** advances early-fluent readers toward fluency through increased text and concept load, less reliance on visuals, longer sentences, and more literary language.

**Level 4** builds reading stamina by providing more text per page, increased use of punctuation, greater variation in sentence patterns, and increasingly challenging vocabulary.

**Level 5** encourages children to move from "learning to read" to "reading to learn" by providing even more text, varied writing styles, and less familiar topics.

Whichever book is right for your reader, Blastoff! Readers are the perfect books to build confidence and encourage a love of reading that will last a lifetime!

This edition first published in 2019 by Bellwether Media, Inc.

No part of this publication may be reproduced in whole or in part without written permission of the publisher. For information regarding permission, write to Bellwether Media, Inc., Attention: Permissions Department, 6012 Blue Circle Drive, Minnetonka, MN 55343.

Library of Congress Cataloging-in-Publication Data

Names: Bowman, Chris, 1990- author.
Title: Highways / by Chris Bowman.
Description: Minneapolis, MN : Bellwether Media, Inc., 2019. | Series:
   Blastoff! Readers. Everyday Engineering | Includes bibliographical
   references and index. | Audience: Ages 5-8. | Audience: Grades K to 3.
Identifiers: LCCN 2018000218 (print) | LCCN 2018001456 (ebook) | ISBN
   9781626178236 (hardcover : alk. paper) | ISBN 9781681035642 (ebook)
Subjects: LCSH: Highway engineering–Juvenile literature.
Classification: LCC TE149 (ebook) | LCC TE149 .B69 2019 (print) | DDC 625.7–dc23
LC record available at https://lccn.loc.gov/2018000218

Editor: Paige V. Polinsky     Designer: Jeffrey Kollock

Printed in the United States of America, North Mankato, MN

# Table of Contents

# What Are Highways?

Highways are major roads that run between cities and towns.

They allow cars and trucks to drive quickly between places.

Many early roads were made of sand and stone. Others used wood or brick.

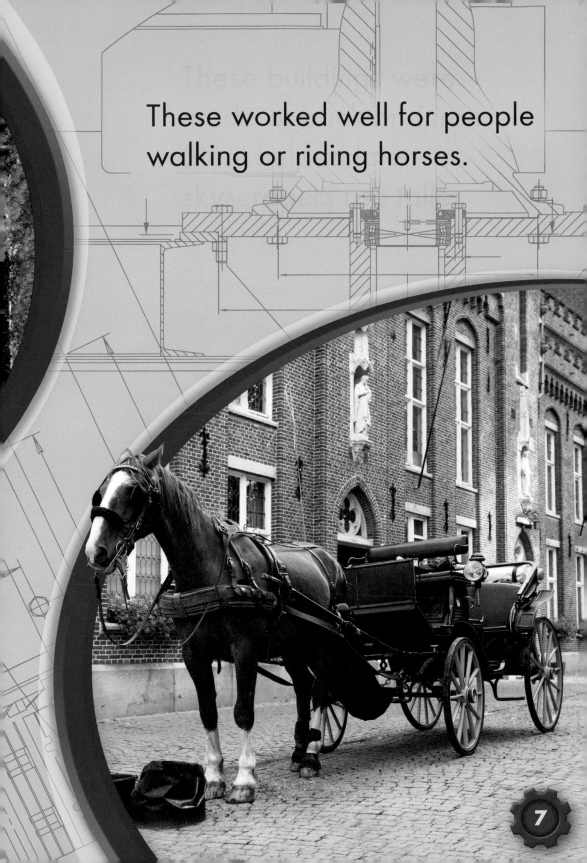

These worked well for people walking or riding horses.

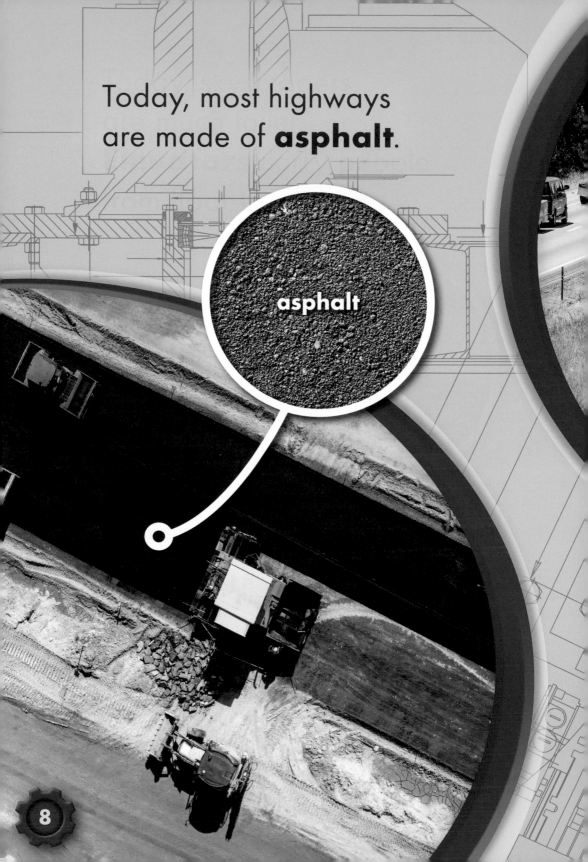

Today, most highways
are made of **asphalt**.

asphalt

This is strong enough to hold the **load** of cars and trucks.

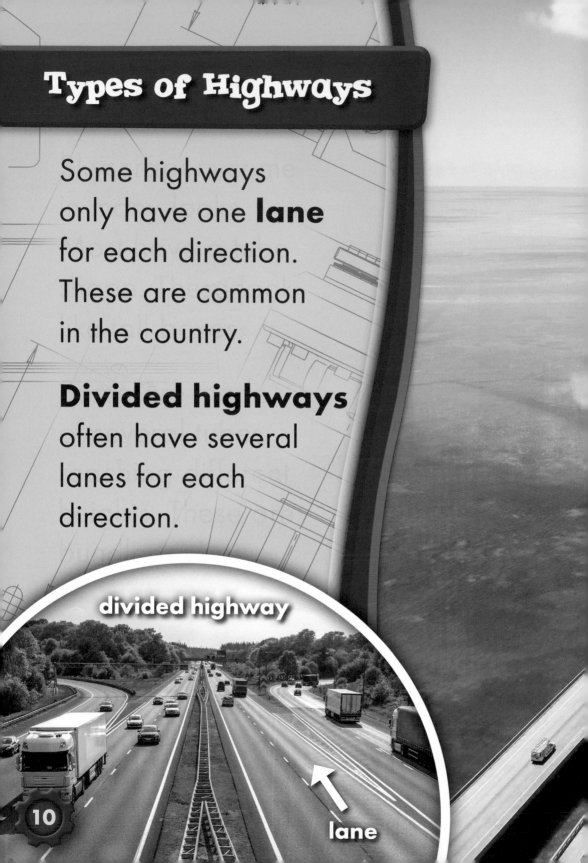

# Types of Highways

Some highways only have one **lane** for each direction. These are common in the country.

**Divided highways** often have several lanes for each direction.

divided highway

lane

**FAMOUS STRUCTURE PROFILE**

# Overseas Highway

**Location:** Florida Keys

**Type:** two-lane highway

**Year Completed:** 1938

**Engineer:** B.M. Duncan

**Length:** 113 miles (182 kilometers)

expressway
intersection

**Expressways** allow high speeds. Cars often enter on ramps. Some expressways **intersect** other roads.

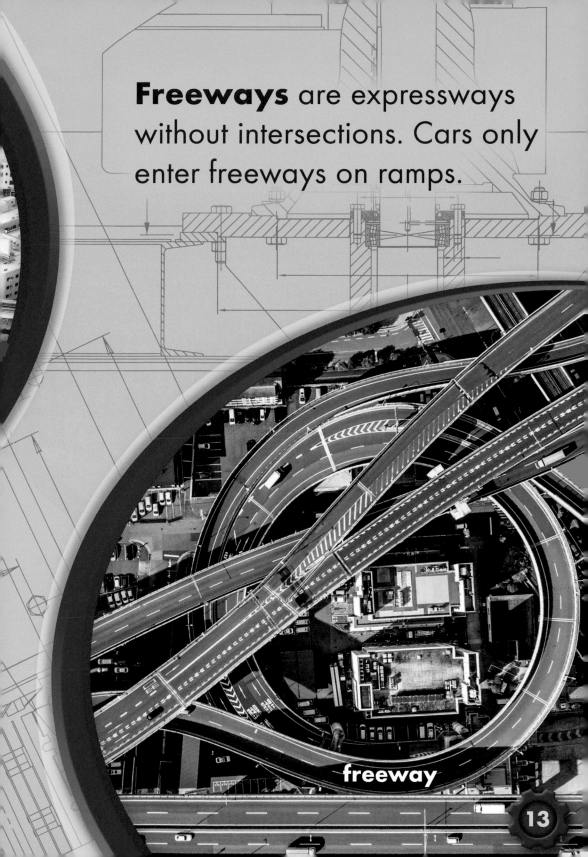

**Freeways** are expressways without intersections. Cars only enter freeways on ramps.

freeway

It costs money to use some highways. Tollways charge drivers at points along the road.

**tollway**

This money often helps
build new highways.

# How Do Highways Work?

**Engineers** pick paths for highways. They consider each road's main use.

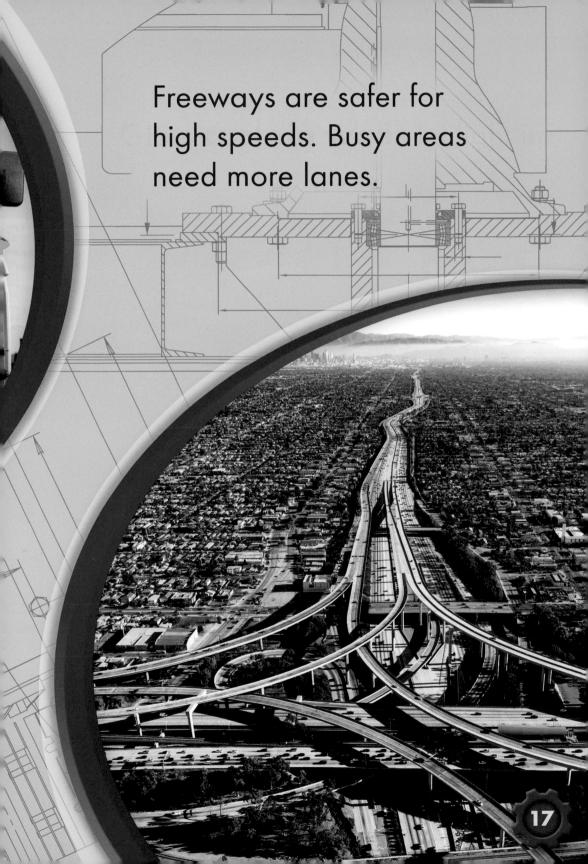

Freeways are safer for high speeds. Busy areas need more lanes.

# Friction at Work

tire

friction   pavement

Rough **pavement** gives highways extra **friction**. This keeps tires from slipping.

Stone, sand, and steel **support** the pavement from below.

stone and sand

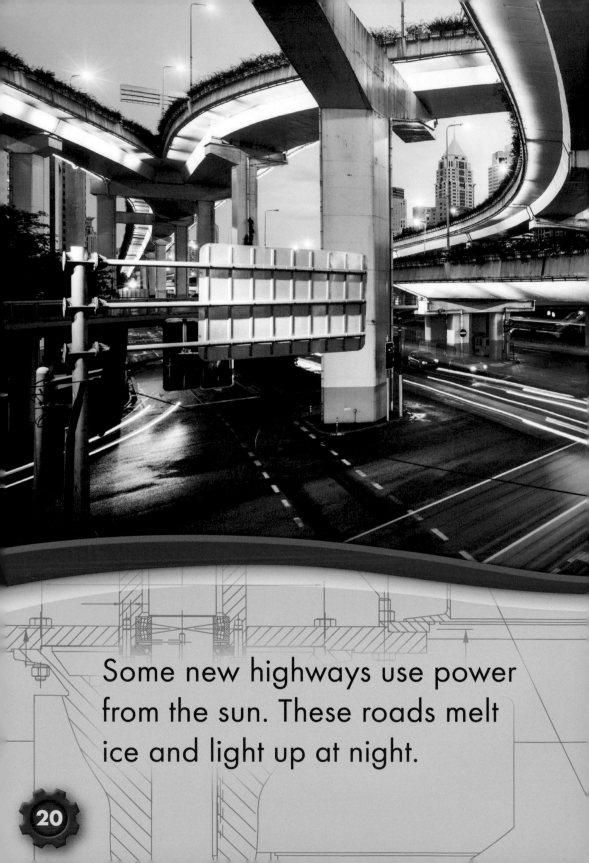

Some new highways use power from the sun. These roads melt ice and light up at night.

They help us stay
safe at high speeds!

# Glossary

**asphalt**—a hard building material made of dark sand and gravel

**divided highways**—major roads that use a wall or strip of land to separate lanes moving in opposite directions

**engineers**—designers and builders of structures or machines

**expressways**—divided highways that allow for high speeds; cars may enter expressways through intersections or on ramps.

**freeways**—expressways without intersections; cars must enter freeways on ramps.

**friction**—a force between two objects as they rub against one another

**intersect**—to cross; intersections are places where two or more roads cross one another, often using stoplights or stop signs.

**lane**—a strip of road used for a single line of cars

**load**—weight or pressure

**pavement**—the hard surface of a highway; pavement is often made of asphalt.

**support**—to help hold something up

# To Learn More

**AT THE LIBRARY**

Doudna, Kelly. *Building Route 66.*
Minneapolis, Minn.: ABDO Pub., 2018.

Furgang, Kathy. *Zoom in on Superhighways.*
New York, N.Y.: Enslow Publishing, 2018.

Proudfit, Benjamin. *The Pacific Coast Highway.*
New York, N.Y.: Gareth Stevens Pub., 2017.

**ON THE WEB**

Learning more about
highways is as easy as 1, 2, 3.

1. Go to www.factsurfer.com.

2. Enter "highways" into the search box.

3. Click the "Surf" button and you will see a
   list of related web sites.

With factsurfer.com, finding more information is
just a click away.

# Index

The images in this book are reproduced through the courtesy of: Pipochka, front cover; chrupka, front cover; Color4260, front cover, pp. 2-3, 22-24; Bubushonok, front cover, pp. 4-24 (blueprint background); darin.k, pp. 4-24 (gears); Blue Planet Studio, pp. 4-5; Predrag Lukic, pp. 6-7; Philippe Put, p. 7; Stockr, p. 8; VMCgroup, p. 8 (inset); Carolyn Franks, pp. 8-9; Rudmer Zwerver, p. 10; Mia2you, pp. 10-11; GagliardiImages, pp. 12-13; Avigator Thailand, p. 13; Ilya Osovetskiy, p. 14; jocic, pp. 14-15; cate_89, pp. 16-17; TierneyMJ, p. 17; dymentyd, p. 18; supergenijalac, pp. 18-19; Noppharat4969, p. 19 (inset); Roland Nagy/ Alamy, pp. 20-21.